easy flowers

easy flowers

Jane Durbridge & Antonia Swinson

photography by Polly Wreford

Ideas for every room in your home

RYLAND
PETERS
& SMALL
LONDON NEW YORK

To Stephen, Mark, and Claire

DESIGNER Luis Peral-Aranda
COMMISSIONING EDITOR Annabel Morgan
EDITOR Sharon Ashman
LOCATION RESEARCH Claire Hector
PRODUCTION Tamsin Curwood
ART DIRECTOR Gabriella Le Grazie
PUBLISHING DIRECTOR Alison Starling

FLOWER STYLING Jane Durbridge
TEXT Antonia Swinson

First published in 2003.
This edition published in 2010 by
Ryland Peters & Small
20–21 Jockey's Fields
London WC1R 4BW
and
519 Broadway
5th Floor
New York, NY 10012

www.rylandpeters.com

ISBN: 978-1-84597-985-0

10 9 8 7 6 5 4 3 2 1

Text, design and photographs copyright
© Ryland Peters & Small 2003 and 2010

A CIP record for this book is available from the British
Library.

The original edition of this book was cataloged as follows:

Library of Congress Cataloging-in-Publication Data

Durbridge, Jane.
  Easy flowers : ideas for every room in your home / Jane
Durbridge and Antonia Swinson ; photography by Polly Wreford.
    p. cm.
  ISBN 1-84172-398-3
  1. Flower arrangement. I. Swinson, Antonia. II. Title.
  SB449 .D85 2003
  745.92--dc21
                              2002151223

Printed and bound in China

contents

introduction

This is a book about how *not* to arrange flowers. In other words, it's full of ideas so simple that anyone should be able to copy them, whether or not they've arranged flowers before. Traditionally, flower arranging has followed strict rules over such things as the correct height of flowers in relation to their container and so on. I've tried to show here that modern flower arranging needn't adhere to restrictive rules and that no specialized skills are necessary. All you need is enthusiasm and a willingness to experiment.

Fresh flowers are a joyous and uplifting addition to any home. There was a time when cut flowers were only available from florists and were considered something of a luxury. Nowadays they are available at affordable prices from all sorts of convenient places—supermarkets, your corner store, even gas/petrol stations. You won't find the same breadth of choice in all these places, of course, and some of the more unusual and exotic flowers will only be available from florists. However, it's nearly always possible to find stalwarts such as roses, chrysanthemums, carnations, tulips, and lilies anywhere that flowers are sold. None of the arrangements in this book are expensive, and in many cases they use only a few stems, making them as economical as they are beautiful.

But this book isn't just about flowers, it's also about containers and finding a stylish match between the two. We've photographed a huge number of containers—everything from a Pink Panther bathroom glass to one-off designer vases—to show how big the choice is. You may be lucky enough to own a spectacular vase, or you may only have an empty olive oil bottle on hand. Either way, you can have beautiful—and beautifully simple—flowers in your home. And believe me, once you've lived with fresh flowers, you won't ever want to be without them.

Jane Durbridge

flower basics

design principles

When it comes to arranging flowers, the first rule is to choose flowers that you love and will enjoy living with. If you like the way they look, that's good enough. But if you're unsure or unconfident about where to start, use white flowers or foliage alone, either of which will look good in any interior.

Most of the arrangements in this book use a single variety of flower in a single color, a method that is both simple and stylish. If you want a mixed arrangement, you can, of course, buy separate bunches and combine them yourself. If you're not that confident, try buying a ready-mixed bunch from a florist. If it's been hand tied, you've got an instant arrangement, so don't make the mistake of untying it—it'll look much better if you just put it in a container as it is.

A few stems are often enough to make a focal point if you choose flowers with impact such as lilies (*Lilium*), alliums (*Allium*), African lilies (*Agapanthus*), orchids (Orchidaceae family), or delphiniums (*Delphinium*). Using an odd number of stems tends to give a better effect than an even number.

We're spoiled for choice nowadays, as many flowers are available all year round. This has obvious advantages in winter when flowers would otherwise be scarce. However, if you buy according to season, you'll get better value for money and the pleasure of enjoying things at the right time of year: daffodils (*Narcissus*) in spring, for instance, and dahlias or sunflowers during the summer months.

Think twice before you throw out bottles, jars, or anything else that could be used to hold flowers (see page 12 for inspiration). If you're using a mixture of containers (see, for example, the botany table display on page 104), maintain one element of continuity to prevent the effect from being a jumble. In this instance, all the bottles are clear glass and are tall and narrow. A collection of blue glass bottles, teacups, glass jars, or white ceramic containers in different shapes could look equally effective.

Although you shouldn't be inhibited by any notions of flower-arranging rules, a couple of basic guidelines may help you when you're getting started. Large vases with wide necks usually need large arrangements to look their best. You'll get away with a sparser arrangement if a vase is large but narrow necked, or if it's tall and narrow. A round pot usually looks best holding a full, dome-shaped bunch. One of the easiest ways to arrange flowers is to cut the stems so the heads sit just above the rim of the container. This also makes a small bunch look bigger than it is.

If you're experimenting with flower arranging for the first time, start with material from your own backyard or the less expensive bunches stocked by supermarkets so that if you make mistakes they won't be expensive ones. Good luck!

Opposite **Flowers are extraordinarily versatile, lending themselves to formal, graphic treatments such as this one just as readily as they do to more relaxed schemes.** Right **As an alternative to cut flowers, many spring bulbs can be planted indoors for a welcome winter and spring display.**

vases and equipment

TO HAVE AND TO HOLD Finding the right container for a flower display is as important as the arrangement itself. With a bit of imagination, almost anything can be put to stylish use. Vases can, of course, be expensive, but beautiful designer pieces should last a lifetime and can make a big statement in a room. There are, however, a host of cheaper alternatives which, with the right flowers and foliage, can look just as effective. Vintage containers have great charm and can often be picked up secondhand. You may have the opportunity to rummage in relatives' attics or cupboards, and a quick scout around your own home will probably yield olive oil, water, wine, ginger ale, or even perfume bottles, as well as teacups, glass jars, and odd drinking glasses. All of them can be put to creative use.

Opposite **Flower arrangements** needn't involve much time or money. Here, a cylindrical vase and a few stems of ivy (*Hedera helix*) create an instant, chic result. Right **Disguising** flower stems with coffee beans transforms the look of a simple vase.

BITTER SWEET You don't need special materials to create striking displays—a raid on the kitchen provided the starting point for this one. Though hardly a classic combination, chocolate-brown coffee beans and blowsy, ivory Anne Marie roses (*Rosa*) look surprisingly effective together. The contrast in texture and color adds a touch of drama. The roses are trimmed to the height of a small glass vase (a glass jar would also work well) and grouped into a tight cluster. They are then placed in a larger, square vase and the space between the two containers is filled with coffee beans. This vase within a vase technique can be used with many other materials, from pebbles and glass nuggets to dried beans and even slices of fresh fruit.

Left and right **The shape of a vase often suggests a particular shape of arrangement, but there's always more than one way of displaying flowers in a vase. For instance, using long-stemmed flowers in a tall vase will look more formal than allowing their heads to spill over its rim.**

This page **A small round pot is matched by a domed bunch of chincherinchees.**

Top right **The graphic look of this ring-shaped vase finds a good counterpart in the long, curved lines of aspidistra leaves.**

TAKING SHAPE Containers come in all shapes and sizes. Getting the right balance between the shape of your container and the shape of your flowers is a crucial element in an arrangement. For instance, the domed shape of the bunch of Turkish chincherinchees (*Ornithogalum arabicum*) shown left mimics the round pot in which they've been placed. If you've got a tall, narrow container, combining it with long-stemmed flowers—see the alliums (*Allium*) on page 86—makes a very exaggerated, emphatic statement. However, arranging flowers so the heads form a lollipop effect above the rim of a tall vase—see the roses (*Rosa*) on page 51— creates a softer look. Even with very small containers such as teacups there's scope for variety: compare the single poppy anemone (*Anemone coronaria* De Caen Group) on page 83 with the tight posy of roses (*Rosa*) on page 25.

Quirky, unusual containers may inspire you to create living sculptures with your flowers, such as the tightly bound tower of narcissi (*Narcissus*) on page 56, or this ring-shaped vase, above, with an asymmetric formation of aspidistra leaves (*Aspidistra*). Large, cylindrical vases or goldfish bowls allow you to experiment with effects that are designed to be viewed *through* the glass, such as the peonies (*Paeonia*) shown on page 79. Conversely, arrangements in shallow containers may look most effective from above, such as the geometric green chrysanthemums (*Chrysanthemum*) on page 41. The secret is to experiment and have fun doing it.

BOLD CONTRASTS A container can either contrast with or complement its contents. As this show-stopping display of parrot tulips (*Tulipa*) shows, right, some containers seem to cry out for a particular flower. Taking a different approach, the orange gerberas (*Gerbera*) on page 33 have been placed on blue-black plates for a deliberate color counterpoint. The lilac-pink sweet peas (*Lathyrus odoratus*) in a pale green vase, left, are also a contrasting combination, but a far gentler one. For the greatest flexibility, clear glass or white ceramic provide neutral backdrops that work with any color. Galvanized pots are also versatile, while black containers add drama and usually work best with a strong hue—such as red—or, of course, white.

Above **Whether you decide on subtle or powerful combinations will depend on your mood, your home's décor, and what's available at the time. The great thing about using fresh flowers is the fact that they're temporary and can be replaced with a different arrangement in an instant.**
Right **Clear, white, or pale containers are the easiest and most versatile to work with.**

Right **Sometimes the choice of flower determines the choice of container, but at other times a striking container will inspire an arrangement itself. Here, a spectacular vase was the starting point and the flowers naturally followed.**
Far right **Only a few pieces of inexpensive equipment are needed to create the displays in this book.**

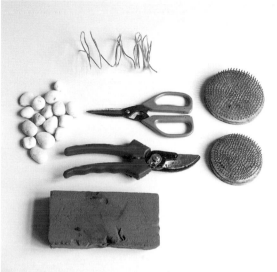

EQUIPMENT You need very little paraphernalia to reproduce the arrangements in this book. However, a few easily obtainable items will be useful. Sharp kitchen scissors cut most plant stems, and shears will deal with anything tougher, such as branches of blossom. Florist's wire is useful for tying and binding— see the pussy willow display on page 120, for instance—but raffia or garden twine will often do instead. Pebbles can be used in table decorations or to top dress pots (see pages 45 and 46) and can be bought from home improvement/DIY stores or garden centers. Pin holders, available from florists, are an old-fashioned but effective device for anchoring plant stems (see the gerberas on page 111). Finally, although I haven't used it in this book, florist's foam is also handy for anchoring plant stems, particularly in shallow containers.

flower palettes

yellows

SPRING SUNSHINE Dwarf daffodils (*Narcissus*), along with their larger sisters, make a welcome appearance in late winter and early spring, brightening up the garden with their cheerful flowers. Bulbs are available in garden centers or by mail order through specialized suppliers, and can be planted in all manner of containers for an indoor display. For this conservatory a rich, golden yellow variety called Tête-à-tête has been grown in small galvanized pots, top dressed with moss. Many winter- and spring-flowering bulbs can be grown indoors, among them scented paper-white narcissi (*Narcissus papyraceus*) and hyacinths (*Hyacinthus*), dwarf tulips (*Tulipa*) and irises (*Iris reticulata*), and crocuses (*Crocus*).

Just one type of dwarf daffodil has been grown here, but you could experiment with a mixture. There are many beautiful varieties—ranging from cream to bright yellow—including some, such as geranium narcissi (see page 107), with white petals and orange cups.

This page and bottom right **Although yellow is a hot, energizing hue, it needn't be strident. In both of these arrangements, its warmth has been** tempered by the presence of cooler tones in the containers—a stone-effect pot and a blue and white vintage teacup and saucer.

MELLOW YELLOW This pretty arrangement could be given as a present or used as a place marker at a dinner party. Yellow spray roses (*Rosa*), some just opening, some in bud, have been cut short and placed in a vintage teacup and saucer. The idea could be adapted for a small wedding reception by putting posies, tied with pretty ribbon, in guests' glasses so they can be taken home at the end of the day. If you wanted to use this type of arrangement as place markers, you could experiment with variations on the theme. Using one type of rose and one pattern of china throughout produces an elegant, coordinated look, but you could give each guest a different type of rose and teacup for an attractively eclectic effect.

A small, compact bunch of yellow roses has found a home in a stone-effect garden pot, placed by a basin in a bathroom. Effective flower arrangements are often as much about texture as they are about color and here the addition of cobwebby Spanish moss (*Tillandsia usneoides*) produces a soft-focus feel. The wispy, gossamer-light moss echoes the delicacy of the rose petals themselves, making this a pretty and feminine arrangement. The cool neutral shade of the pot, which reflects the surface on which it sits, work surprisingly well with the warmer tones of the flowers, creating a display that is pleasing and restful on the eye.

oranges

BIG AND BOLD Sometimes you'll find a flower so irresistible that it cries out to be taken home and put on show. At other times the inspiration will come from elsewhere, and in this case it's a spectacular tall glass vase, shaded from deep red through vermilion to tangerine. Filling it with deep orange parrot tulips (*Tulipa*), flamed with red, is a marriage made in heaven. Arranging the flowers with the heads spilling over the rim of the vase balances the height of the display and focuses attention on the intricate markings on the ruffled petals. An arrangement as dramatic and vibrant as this needs the right sort of backdrop, and this living room, with its neutral walls and large orange painting (by Mark Upton), complements rather than competes with it.

Tulips are an invaluable ingredient in the flower arranger's palette. They have a strong and beautiful form, last well, are good value for money, and can be found in almost every color of the rainbow—true blue being about the only exception.

Orange strikes a sunny
and uplifting note against
a pristine white backdrop.
With darker colors it
acquires a more grown-up,
glamorous air. Here, parrot
tulips (*Tulipa*) in all the
shades of a sunset have
been placed in a shiny,
black ceramic vase and
provide a shot of searing
color alongside the
dark furniture.

STATELY HOME Crown imperials (*Fritillaria imperialis*), left, are majestic flowers, their topknots of slender leaves above vermilion bells giving them the appearance of miniature palm trees. Placing them in a curvy, dark brown glass vase shows off their height and creates a show-stopping arrangement, even when using only five stems. Flowers as unusual as this look most effective in a room whose décor won't be overshadowed by their flair. Here, they are flanked by strong lines in the shape of dark bookcases and large, masculine chairs.

Crown imperials aren't for everyone—apart from their quirky looks, they have an earthy smell that some people find disagreeable. They could be replaced by blue or white African lilies (*Agapanthus*) or alliums (*Allium*, see page 87) for an equally eye-catching arrangement.

Left **It takes confidence to use flowers as tall and unusual as these in the home. However, arranged in a striking vase and placed where they'll command attention, they look wonderful.**

CITRUS ZEST For creating stunning, yet simple arrangements, gerberas (*Gerbera*) are almost too good to be true. Their large blooms are pretty and open, and come in a vibrant array of shades—particularly yellows, oranges, reds, and pinks. They are bold and beautiful, and last extremely well. Here, a burnt-orange variety contrasts with a dark wooden table and deep blue china to create an uncomplicated, lively display for a dinner party. A shallow vase with three separate compartments holds individual blooms, their stems cut short, with the addition of some papyrus stems (*Cyperus papyrus*), right, as an accent. More gerberas decorate the plates, and a bowl piled high with ripe oranges ties the decorative scheme together.

The combination of dark brown, blue, and orange is a bold and sophisticated one. Orange also works well with other colors at the warm end of the spectrum, such as red and yellow, or as a foil to dazzling white.

English pot marigolds have been in cultivation for hundreds of years and possess an unpretentious simplicity that is hard to resist.

SWEET ORANGE A rough wooden headboard and cabinet set a rustic tone in this bedroom. Pot marigolds (*Calendula officinalis*) are a classic cottage-garden flower and match the mood perfectly. They are some of the easiest annuals to grow and will bloom obligingly throughout the summer. Sow a pack of seeds in the spring, and you'll have enough flowers to adorn your home and garden all season. Marigolds vary from cream and apricot to rich yellow and bright orange, with double as well as single forms.

Here, a small tied bunch—some of them in flower, some in bud—have been popped into a smoky-glass cube vase, along with a few of their leaves, for the simplest of arrangements. If marigolds aren't to your taste on display in the house, they may be to your taste in the kitchen—the petals are edible (as long as they haven't been sprayed) and look wonderful added to a salad.

greens

Right **Though they are traditional items of garden paraphernalia, galvanized buckets have been given a new lease on life by modern florists. This tiny one is just the right size for a frothy dome of mind-your-own-business.**

GREEN HOUSE Mind-your-own-business (*Soleirolia*) can be found in three different shades—dark green, lime green, and variegated. All have tiny, round leaves that form plump, frothy "cushions" and can be grown both indoors and out.

In the home, mind-your-own-business looks good almost anywhere—next to a basin in the bathroom, on a kitchen windowsill, lined up on a living-room mantelpiece or, as here, as an attractive addition to a dinner table. Plants in all three color forms have been placed in small, chunky glass vases along the length of a low, wooden table. The oriental tableware and white walls reinforce the room's contemporary, minimal look, and the neat green domes of leaves bring a touch of light relief to this slightly austere setting. Mind-your-own-business, like ornamental grasses (see pages 44—45), makes a very effective table arrangement because its tactile quality invites guests to run their hands over its leaves.

LIME LIGHT These green goddess chrysanthemums (*Chrysanthemum*) are extraordinary in form and color. Their fine, lime-green petals curl over to produce pompomlike blooms which, even used sparingly, give instant impact. Here, a shallow, square glass vase has been covered with a lattice made from horsetail (*Equisetum hyemale*), which can be secured in position with reusable adhesive tack or transparent adhesive tape. The flower stems have been stripped of their leaves and cut short. The heads can then be arranged in any pattern that appeals—straight or diagonal lines, for instance. Alternatively, each square can be filled with a flower. This clean, cool arrangement looks particularly good in a bathroom, or perhaps in a minimal white kitchen. Other plants that could be used this way are full roses (*Rosa*), tulips (*Tulipa*), or gerberas (*Gerbera*).

Lime green strikes
a fresh note and
looks particularly
good in a light and
airy setting such as
this white bathroom.
It is a hue more
commonly seen on
foliage than flowers,
but there are a few
lime-green flowers
to be found, such as
green tulips (*Tulipa*)
and zinnia (*Zinnia*),
and lady's mantle
(*Alchemilla mollis*) .

NEW LEAF Leaves can be just as beautiful as flowers and are a subject matter for arrangements in their own right. This shallow black bowl, above, is tailormade for a minimal display with oriental overtones. A couple of ligularia leaves (*Ligularia*) have been tucked among a few round pebbles to anchor them. These leaves won't last as long as foliage with longer stems, but something this simple can be freshened up in a moment with any type of large, attractive leaf.

Garden trees and shrubs provide a rich source of material for arrangements. Look for branches with interesting shapes like this one, right, which has been cut from a kiwi shrub (*Actinidia deliciosa*) and placed in an amphora-shaped vase. Sprigs of leaves can also be used. Top right, kiwi has been used again, popped into a Japanese cup to give a display of zenlike simplicity. Bottom right, a length of Virginia creeper (*Parthenocissus quinquefolia*) has been placed in an empty olive oil bottle. Such a simple display proves that, with a little imagination, almost any plant or, indeed, container can be used.

Leaf shapes vary enormously. On these pages, rounded and heart-shaped foliage has been used to produce a soft and tranquil effect. Long, thin leaves, such as those used on pages 44—45, create a more vibrant, energizing result.

STRAIGHT AND NARROW Left, papyrus (*Cyperus papyrus*) is hardly a common or garden plant, but you'll find it in some florists. Its long, straight stems, finishing in tufts of straplike leaves, are at once graceful and emphatic. Arranged in a narrow-necked, smoky-glass vase, the stems give this room a colonial air. Papyrus is a practical as well as elegant choice since it is long-lasting and also looks good when dry. If it's not available, African lily (*Agapanthus*), bulrushes (*Typha latifolia*), or one of any number of grasses would give a similar effect.

This page, sedges (*Scirpus cernuus*)—bought in pots from garden centers—form tufts of fine blades that call out to be stroked. This tactile quality makes them ideal table decorations. Here, they've been given an oriental treatment by being placed in small black and white ceramic bowls with a top dressing of pale and dark pebbles.

Opposite **Papyrus is an exotic choice of plant and makes an impressive focal point in this simple, modern interior. This page Grasses have become an essential component of modern garden design, and there's no reason why they shouldn't be used inside as well.**

TALL STORY Stems can play as important a role as flowers in an arrangement. These Turkish chincherinchees (*Ornithogalum arabicum*) stand tall in a cylindrical glass vase, anchored in a pin holder that has been disguised with black pebbles. The long, slender stems topped with small, white flowers are an elegant grouping and look particularly graceful placed where the natural light can filter through them.

Opposite, these extraordinary seed heads look almost like decorated beads and are formed by a variety of tulip (*Tulipa*). Seed heads have long been an essential part of the flower arranger's palette, particularly at times of the year when flowers are not in abundance. Their architectural quality is emphasized here by a striking black-and-white vase. The vase's elliptical pattern makes an effective counterpart to the stripes of the seed heads and gives the arrangement an ethnic look.

Opposite **Color takes a back seat in this stylish arrangement, accepting second place to structure and silhouette.** This page **These seed heads are so decorative they could have been painted.**

whites

MODERN ROMANCE Two branches of cherry blossom (*Prunus*) say it all, heralding spring with style. This elegant and spare arrangement—housed in a tall wood-grained earthenware vase—has oriental overtones, echoing the Japanese love affair with the cherry tree. The arching branches and their delicate white blooms are graceful and feminine, and can be found on many suburban streets. Branches from other flowering trees could, of course, be used—apple (*Malus*) perhaps, or pear (*Pyrus*).

This page **Twigs from the garden, held on a blank wall with picture pins and reusable adhesive tack, make a new way to say it with flowers. This piece of original art was created by Laurent Bayard. Such an arrangement could be put up quickly as a surprise for an anniversary, birthday, or homecoming, and just as easily changed or removed. To partner it, ivory roses (*Rosa*)—which could be substituted with peonies (*Paeonia*) or tulips (*Tulipa*)—peep over the rim of a tall square vase.**
Opposite **This painting is by Mark Upton.**

PURE ELEGANCE Phalaenopsis orchids (*Phalaenopsis*) are exquisitely ornamental flowers. Despite their fragile good looks and exotic origins, they make very successful indoor plants and flower for long periods of time. Pot-grown plants can be bought from any good florist (or even in some supermarkets) to make an instant focal point that will outlast any cut flower.

Above left and below left, this phalaenopsis sits on a mantelpiece in a container smothered with silver disks, which complement the orchid's rounded petals and reflect their snowy whiteness. A skeletal twig has been added to the pot, emphasizing the plant's sculptural quality. Above and opposite, a tall galvanized bucket makes an elegant alternative home, with twisted bamboo striking an oriental note.

With their stately and sophisticated air, these phalaenopsis orchids look at home in a modern, unfussy interior. Phalaenopsis are originally from the tropics, but they'll grow happily as house plants and are tougher than their looks suggest.

The best things in life
are free, so when
you're looking for
material for flower
arranging, why not
start in your own
backyard? Cow
parsley, this page,
often thrives in
unkempt corners,
or you may be
lucky enough to have
a flowering tree in
your yard to provide
you with spring
blossom, opposite.

COUNTRY CHARM We've all seen cow parsley (*Anthriscus sylvestris*) in flower along country lanes, covered in clouds of tiny white blooms, but it's so useful in floristry that it's now also grown commercially. Wildflowers are easy to overlook, but they have an unpretentious charm and are simple to grow from seed in a corner of the garden. Opposite, cow parsley has been gathered into a large, informal bunch, creating a light and airy arrangement. It's been placed in an unlikely container—a plastic shopping bag—and displayed in an empty fireplace. This page, more cherry blossom (*Prunus*), this time arranged in a glass vase big enough to stand on the floor. Several branches have been used to give a loose, abundant look.

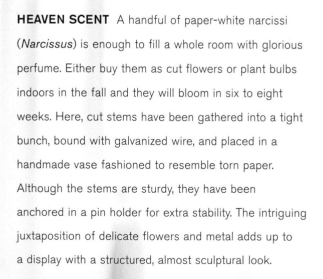

HEAVEN SCENT A handful of paper-white narcissi (*Narcissus*) is enough to fill a whole room with glorious perfume. Either buy them as cut flowers or plant bulbs indoors in the fall and they will bloom in six to eight weeks. Here, cut stems have been gathered into a tight bunch, bound with galvanized wire, and placed in a handmade vase fashioned to resemble torn paper. Although the stems are sturdy, they have been anchored in a pin holder for extra stability. The intriguing juxtaposition of delicate flowers and metal adds up to a display with a structured, almost sculptural look.

Serene and restful, white is easy to live with. It's hard to go wrong with an arrangement of white flowers—they'll create a little oasis of calm in any room. Even in late winter, you can make a delightful little arrangement with a bunch of snowdrops (*Galanthus*), the small, scented flowers offering the same sort of shy prettiness as lily-of-the-valley.

PURE AND SIMPLE Lily-of-the-valley (*Convallaria majalis*) is a plant of exquisite beauty and delicacy with tiny, scented, belllike flowers. You'll find it blooming outdoors in the spring, and it's also grown commercially for florists. It is expensive to buy as a cut flower, but even a tiny pot of it, like the one here, brings elegance to a living space. Because lily-of-the-valley's blooms are so small and fragile, it's a plant that's best used on its own, allowing the flowers to work their own quiet charm. The Victorians were very fond of lily-of-the-valley, and in the language of flowers coined during this period, the plant represented sweetness, simplicity, and purity.

Although these two arrangements use a single type of flower, different shades of white sit very happily together. Using combinations of different white flowers in an arrangement is an easy and foolproof way to use them in the home.

Tulips give their money's worth as a cut flower and provide a long-lasting show. These tulips are the classic shape, but there are other shapes, such as parrot tulips with extravagantly frilled petals (see page 28) and lily tulips with pointed petals.

WHITER SHADES OF PALE White comes in myriad variations and can be dazzling, creamy, or tinged with pink, yellow, green, or blue. Opposite, these roses (*Rosa*) are a warm white with yellow and pink undertones, and provide a bold contrast to a black leather-effect vase. They've been cut so their stems can't be seen above the rim of the vase, focusing the eye on the full, voluptuous blooms. The same roses have been used to decorate place settings and sit on pieces of slate surrounded by a scattering of white pebbles, creating a look that is a mixture of oriental restraint and pure romanticism.

This page, these snowy white tulips (*Tulipa*), packed into a chunky square vase, look quietly chic in this monotone interior. Tulips change in character as their blooms age. Newly open, as here, their ovoid shape looks sleek and modern; as they open more fully, they assume a more romantic form.

EDWARD LUCIE-SMITH and ELISABETH FRINK

PAITS

NPG

blues and purples

BATHING BEAUTY Even the smallest space benefits from flowers. Here it's a bathroom window, where a tiny white vase of bachelor's buttons/cornflowers (*Centaurea cyanus*) joins some knicknacks to create a quirky display. Blue always looks fresh and clean in a bathroom, particularly when partnered with white.

Opposite, flower arranging should be nothing if not fun. Water-retaining crystals, which can be bought in garden centers, are usually added to the mixture in pots to keep the soil moist. Here, however, they've been used to create a soft-focus effect in a large, cylindrical vase. Water was poured onto the crystals, creating a soft gel into which flower heads were pressed. The result is misty, magical, and far removed from more traditional ideas of flower arranging. For this technique to work well, use flowers that are robust and compact in form.

Bachelor's buttons/cornflowers are the very essence of summer. They bring charm to any arrangement and also last well. Here, there are two very different treatments. On this page, a few stems lend a pretty touch to a bathroom window, while opposite, heads "float" in a sea of translucent gel.

Far left **The English woodland bluebell is one of the great joys of spring and suits a simple treatment such as this one.**
Left and right **The beauty of grape hyacinths' sky-blue cones of flowers is worth appreciating in close-up. This interesting technique would also work well with hyacinths (*Hyacinthus*), tulips (*Tulipa*), or bluebells.**

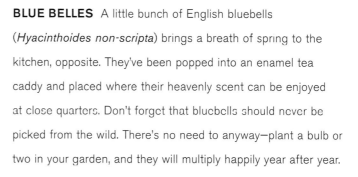

BLUE BELLES A little bunch of English bluebells (*Hyacinthoides non-scripta*) brings a breath of spring to the kitchen, opposite. They've been popped into an enamel tea caddy and placed where their heavenly scent can be enjoyed at close quarters. Don't forget that bluebells should never be picked from the wild. There's no need to anyway—plant a bulb or two in your garden, and they will multiply happily year after year.

Grape hyacinths (*Muscari*), like bluebells, are spring-flowering bulbs. The slightly magnifying effect of glass, left, brings out the intricate beauty of their tightly clustered flowers which, if they are barely opened when first cut or bought, will last for ages. A large bunch has been packed into a hurricane vase, above, with just enough water to give the plants a drink without making the leaves and stems soggy.

SWEET DREAMS Though not as long-lasting as some cut flowers, sweet peas (*Lathyrus odoratus*) more than compensate with their sheer beauty. Their delicate, ruffled petals and mouthwatering shades make them one of the most feminine and romantic flowers, and many varieties have the additional delight of scent. Opposite and inset, a bunch of lilac-pink sweet peas in a green glass vase sits prettily in a bedroom. The two colors are a contrasting combination, but in shades as soft as this, the effect is gentle rather than stimulating. Sweet peas are available from florists, but the plants are easily grown from seed and look charming scrambling up a trellis or wigwam. As with all annual flowers, regular cutting will encourage more blooms and provide a bountiful crop all summer.

Sweet peas come in a wide variety of shades, from white, pastel pinks, and lilacs to bright reds, purples, and purplish-black. Using a single shade, as here, produces an elegant effect, but a mixed bunch will create a less sophisticated, cottage-garden look.

FROM THE HEART A pink, heart-shaped box holding a nosegay of deep purple violas (*Viola*) makes a delightfully romantic Valentine's gift. Halved yogurt pots filled with water hold the flowers in the open box. Alternatively, the violas could be tied into a posy with ribbon and placed on top of the box, perhaps with the addition of a layer of tempting chocolates inside. Violas and sweet violets (*Viola odorata*) were beloved by the Victorians and appear to be enjoying a resurgence of popularity with modern gardeners. However, if they're unavailable, dainty snowdrops (*Galanthus*) would make an equally pretty and romantic alternative.

Violas have an old-fashioned charm and make a romantic posy. The plants can be bought as cut flowers or in little pots from a garden center. If they're kept in their containers, they can be planted outside later.

COOL AND CALM Irises (*Iris*) are elegant flowers and, combined with powder-blue hyacinths (*Hyacinthus*), create a tranquil pool of blue in this living room. They've been arranged in a blueish-purple glass vase with aspidistra leaves (*Aspidistra*) wrapped around it for extra interest. The exquisite yellow markings on the irises' graceful petals inject a little contrast into the scheme. Irises are a huge family of flowers whose varieties come in a rainbow of colors, from snowy white to almost black. However, those grown commercially are usually shades of rich blue, purple, yellow, or white. Some types of iris are scented, though here it's the deliciously heady perfume of the hyacinths that dominates the partnership.

Hyacinths and dwarf varieties of iris can be grown indoors for a winter display.

Opposite and above
right **If your garden
hydrangeas aren't as
intensely blue as this
one, special products
are available from
garden centers that
can be applied to
the soil to deepen the
color of the flowers.**

Above **The stems of
these dark blue irises
(Iris) have been left
almost full length
and placed in a tall,
sapphire-blue glass
vase. A few stems of
supple willow (Salix)
have been wrapped
around the container
to emphasize the
arrangement's height.**

THE BIG BLUE Opposite and above, this heavy-based, dark
blue glass vase is chunky enough to carry off two huge heads
of mophead hydrangea (*Hydrangea macrophylla*), which can
be found in florists and is also a popular garden plant. For this
arrangement, a decorative "handle" of Virginia creeper
(*Parthenocissus quinquefolia*) has been bound with florist's
wire—you could use fine twine or raffia instead—and tucked into
the top of the vase. Stems of ivy (*Hedera helix*) or any other
climber could be used to the same effect. Hydrangeas are
valuable flowers indoors not only for their size and color; they
also last well when cut and take on a fragile beauty as they dry.

pinks

The pointed buds of the lotus flower—like little snakes' heads rising above the vase—are as interesting as the fully opened blooms.

HOT TROPICS Although flower arrangements are often the result of considerable time, effort, and skill, they're sometimes the product of happy accidents. These five stems of lotus (*Nelumbo*) happened to fall to one side when placed in an oval vase, creating an interesting shape, so that's where they were left. With their sinuous stems and hot-pink blooms, the flowers exude an exotic flair. They're not always easy to find, but calla lilies (*Zantedeschia aethiopica*) or oriental lilies (*Lilium auratum*) would give a similarly bold, tropical effect. Although all these flowers are more expensive than those more commonly used in floristry—such as carnations (*Dianthus*) and roses (*Rosa*)—a few stems are all that's needed to create a striking focal point. Above and above right, two more lotus flowers rest on a tropical leaf, bringing added interest to an Eastern-style table setting. Although flowers out of water have a limited life, spritzing them regularly with cold water will get the most out of them.

SHEER PRETTINESS This large hurricane vase, opposite, makes a spectacular table arrangement for a party. A sheet of clear cellophane, which can be bought from a stationer or florist, has been crumpled inside the vase. Pink peonies (*Paeonia*)—which could be replaced by roses (*Rosa*)—have been tucked down into it before adding water, producing a cracked-ice effect. Flowers that have been submerged like this won't last as long as those that have only their stems in water, but they should look good for a day or so. To finish, peonies have been used to dress place settings, above right, and a smaller arrangement has been created by piling peonies and limes on a plate, above center.

Above **Take a look at your tableware in the kitchen and plan your choice of flowers around it to give a pleasingly coordinated look.** Opposite **Here, a palette of sugary pinks and zesty greens—which extends to china, flowers, glasses, and napkins—ties the whole table arrangement together.**

DINING IN PINK This unashamedly romantic table scheme celebrates pink in its most mouthwatering forms with peonies (*Paeonia*), roses (*Rosa*), and Singapore orchids (*Dendrobium*) in shades from candyfloss to fuchsia. A large goldfish bowl, filled with water and huge blooms, and surrounded by silky petals, makes a spectacular arrangement. It is echoed by floating flower heads in water and wine glasses at each place setting and a scattering of petals on the plates and table. The overall effect is pretty, soft, and summery—a guaranteed talking point at a dinner party. If you use scented roses, another sensory element is added to the composition. When flowers play as big a role as this, it's fun to plan a menu that complements the scheme. Here, for instance, bowls of iced borscht, plates of prosciutto and ripe figs, and dishes piled high with succulent summer berries would work well.

This idea could be adapted to suit all sorts of flowers and color schemes. You could try a tranquil green and white palette with variegated foliage and white spray chrysanthemums (*Dendranthema*), for instance, or fragrant sweet peas (*Lathyrus odoratus*) in mixed sugared-almond shades.

BEAUTY SPOT Few flowers can compete with poppy anemones (*Anemone coronaria* De Caen Group) and ranunculus (*Ranunculus asiaticus*) for their prettiness and unabashed femininity. Where better to appreciate their beauty, therefore, than on a dresser? For miniature arrangements such as these, a single bloom is often all that's needed, allowing the delicacy of the flower to speak for itself.

Opposite, this narrow-necked Chinese vase and pretty teacup and saucer are dainty and decorative, a perfect match for the anemones' delicately ruffled petals and feathery black centers. Below, these ranunculus could have been used singly, but their tightly furled form has been emphasized by being gathered into a compact posy and placed in a pearly shell.

Cast aside the idea that vases are the only things to put flowers in. Start hunting in your own home and you'll probably unearth all sorts of containers that could be put to use—old perfume bottles, glass jars, even shells and pretty teacups, such as have been used here, and toothbrush holders (see page 98).

Pink is the most feminine color in the florist's palette, but like other colors, it has a variety of moods. Pale, blushing pinks are sugary and pretty, while shocking pink lives up to its name. There are also cool, restful pinks underscored with blue and warm, stimulating pinks tinged with yellow. All are comforting colors to live with, less demanding than red but more welcoming than blue.

Shades of pink from the cool and warm ends of the spectrum don't sit happily together, so they are probably best not mixed in a bunch. Pink usually works beautifully with green, while reds partner pink surprisingly well, too—see the poppy anemones (*Anemone coronaria* De Caen Group) on page 103. Pink also looks good teamed with the cool tones of silver and blue, which is why the blue Chinese vase (left) and the pearly shell on the opposite page make perfect partners for these luscious rose-pink flowers.

LIGHT FANTASTIC Formality is a useful element in creating simple but stylish flower arrangements. This line-up of six tubular purple glass vases and deep pink tulips (*Tulipa*) achieves its impact through regular repetition. Its rigidity is softened, however, by allowing the flowers to arch in different directions, creating a look which is therefore both formal and informal. The effect of light is very pleasing here, too. Reflectiveness is provided by the glossy marble mantelpiece as well as the large mirror, and the natural light is filtered subtly through the smoky glass. Placing flowers by mirrors helps to heighten their impact, not only because they're seen twice, but also because they're seen from a different angle.

Right **These small, neat tulips are particularly well suited to these narrow vases because their stems are strong enough to hold the flower heads well above their rims, but flexible enough to arch attractively.**

Alliums are from the same family as onions and leeks, and are distinguished by large, fluffy heads, held proud on tall, strong stems. The flowers are usually deep pink to purple and also dry well.

FULL CIRCLE

This arrangement
illustrates a happy
marriage between
container and flowers. This
retro-style vase is designed as
a tower of spheres. It could have
been tailormade for the huge, globular
alliums (*Allium*), whose heads are, in fact,
composed of a mass of tiny, starlike flowers. It's not only
shape that gives this display its impact, it's also the height
of the stems and the upright way in which the blooms are
carried. Plants with this sort of form—including crown imperials
(*Fritillaria imperialis*), African lilies (*Agapanthus*), and papyrus
(*Cyperus papyrus*)—are often better used alone, so their
distinctiveness is uncompromised.

reds

Left **Scarlet tulips and a blood-red glass vase create a tone-on-tone look. Using the tulips' dark green leaves adds natural contrast. Widely available for much of the year and reasonably priced, tulips remain an invaluable plant in the florist's repertoire. Rather than trimming the tulips to the height of the vase, the stems have been left long to create an elegantly arching arrangement.**

GIRLIE GLAMOUR Flowers are a reflection of our lifestyles. This arrangement of poppy anemones (*Anemone coronaria* De Caen Group) in a zebra-striped oval vase takes its cue from its owner's black and white wallpaper and fire-engine red high heels. It's glamorous and feminine, like a dash of red lipstick and a sweep of black eyeliner. The display has a graphic quality, emphasized by the anemones' huge black eyes and the stylized shape of the vase, which tapers to a narrow neck. The same container would also look effective filled with any other blooms with strong color and form: shocking-pink poppy anemones, bright yellow tulips (*Tulipa*), or tangerine-orange gerberas (*Gerbera*), for instance.

This rather imposing fireplace seems to cry out for a floral display. These dark, sultry reds contrast dramatically with the neutral tones of the room, producing a sophisticated effect.

LOVE STORY Love-lies-bleeding (*Amaranthus caudatus*) produces intriguingly unusual flowers—graceful tassels of velvety blooms in deepest burgundy. Partnered with roses (*Rosa*) in the same shade, they make an informal but magnificent show on this impressive fireplace. The deliberately eclectic collection of olive oil and ginger-beer bottles proves that the cheapest and most unlikely of containers can look stylish. Using plants with such graceful flowers and fine stems in narrow, clear bottles gives the display a lightness of touch.

DARK BEAUTY Calla lilies (*Zantedeschia aethiopica*) have an extraordinary fluted shape which gives them the appearance of living sculptures. Their sleek and exotic beauty makes them a sophisticated choice of flower for the home. A setting as glamorous as this—the walls are covered in shimmering gold leaf, echoed by gold and terracotta-colored floor tiles—certainly calls for something luxurious. These sumptuously dark, red-black callas fit the bill perfectly.

Although they are expensive, callas can be used sparingly and still create a strong impact. Here, ten stems have been bound together with raffia in two places to create a tall, tight bunch that arches elegantly when placed in its vase. Tying the stems like this produces a stronger shape than if they were arranged separately, which would produce a softer, more romantic display. To match this modern look, lotus leaves (*Nelumbo*) have been wrapped around a vase and secured, again, with raffia—a useful method of disguise if you have a container in need of an instant facelift.

Flowers with silky or velvety petals look particularly sumptuous in dark, sultry hues. In addition to calla lilies, look for roses (*Rosa*), cockscomb (*Celosia*), tulips (*Tulipa*), and winter pansies (*Viola* x *wittrockiana*).

This page **Arranging**
flowers *inside*
containers opens up
all kinds of new and
exciting possibilities.
It's not only round
bowls that can
be used in this way
(see pages 65 and
119 for further
ideas). If callas are
unavailable or beyond
your budget, tulips
(*Tulipa*) could be used
successfully in their
place (see page 98).

SPECIAL EFFECTS Opposite, coiled around the inside of a goldfish bowl, these calla lilies (*Zantedeschia aethiopica*) do indeed look like a school of fish. Here, the stems play as important a role as the flowers, creating an intricate pattern against the glass.

Carnations (*Dianthus*) are a mainstay of the floristry business, and no wonder: they last for ages, are inexpensive, are available all year, and come in a fabulous range of colors. Because they're so widely available, they've suffered from being overused. However, the display below—three pumpkin-shaped candleholders, each filled with a little water and a dome of carnations—shows how pretty they can be.

BOLD AND BEAUTIFUL Left, for a bit of pure, irreverent fun, a small bunch of exuberant glory lilies (*Gloriosa superba*) has been popped into a kitsch Pink Panther toothbrush holder. This tongue-in-cheek approach reflects the replacement of rigid rules in flower arranging with a more relaxed approach.

Below, in a variation on the goldfish-bowl theme (see page 96), red tulips have been wrapped around the inside of a shallow bowl. An arrangement like this will provide new interest every day because tulips continue to grow in water after they've been cut, producing a changing, living display. Bright red isn't an obvious choice for a bathroom, but against the pristine white basin and tiles, it strikes a vibrant and energizing note.

Opposite, strong red can be a bit overwhelming if it is used on its own. The splashes of white on the petals of this pretty dahlia (*Dahlia*) lighten its effect, as do the green buds emerging from the bunch. Choosing variegated flowers is a useful ploy for anyone who wants to experiment with bold shades without going the whole hog.

Passionate and
intense, red doesn't
appeal to everyone.
Used judiciously,
however, it can be
both warming and
uplifting—a good
choice for those
moments when you
need a lift.

Despite the fact that roses are available in a vast array of colors, many as intense as this shade of red, commercial growers have gone one step further and produced fresh, dyed roses in brilliant and unexpected hues—such as electric blue—which can be found at certain florists.

ROLE REVERSAL Giving flowers as a love token is an age-old practice, and roses in particular have been linked with romance since ancient times. Valentine's Day and red roses go hand in hand, but giving flowers needn't be the exclusive preserve of men. This dashing bouquet was designed with a man in mind, a new twist on the classic bunch of a dozen red roses. A copy of the *Financial Times*, tied with a masculine flourish of black raffia, replaces the usual cellophane—and does double duty as useful reading material! It's not hard to see why roses remain the queen of cut flowers—available all year, everywhere from florists to supermarkets and service stations, their range of colors is second to none, and they are robust enough to last extremely well in arrangements.

vibrant
combinations

Pinks, blues, and purples work harmoniously together, particularly when they're at the paler end of the spectrum. They're the quintessential shades of an English summer garden and suggest femininity and old-fashioned romanticism.

SWEET PASTELS Soft pinks and blues combine easily and are restful on the eye, making them a good choice for a place of relaxation such as a bedroom. These blue bachelor's buttons/cornflowers (*Centaurea cyanus*), catnip (*Nepeta*), and pink roses (*Rosa*) look pretty and feminine in a white porcelain Fifties vase on a bedside table. The arrangement is simple, but it has a touch of formality, making it refined and ladylike.

Opposite, inspired by memories of the botany table at school, this series of deliberately mismatched vases and bottles is filled with single stems of wild and garden flowers. Among them are dill (*Anethum graveolens*), African lily (*Agapanthus*), sea holly (*Eryngium*), roses (*Rosa*), herbaceous sage (*Salvia*), and Virginia creeper (*Parthenocissus quinquefolia*). The result is rustic and charming, and can be achieved with minimum effort and cost.

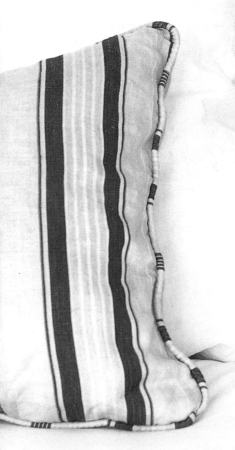

HOUSE WARMING Red and pink don't always work well together, but this informal bunch of ranunculus (*Ranunculus asiaticus*) shows how rich the effect is when they do. Ranunculus are often available from florists in mixed bunches. Here, the flowers have been loosely arranged in a tall white vase on a bedside table and look fresh and summery against the room's pristine white décor. .

Opposite, yellow is the shade we associate with daffodils (*Narcissus*), but this dwarf variety, called geranium, has white outer petals and a deep orange-red cup. A book cover combining orange and red inspired the choice of container for the arrangement—a red glass vase. The combination is warm and uplifting, just right for the time of year when winter's dark days are giving way to spring.

Opposite **There's nothing wrong with letting a florist do some of the work for you and buying a readymade bunch of flowers, such as these mixed ranunculus.**
This page **You may find inspiration where you least expect it— here, a book cover suggested this combination of narcissi and a red glass vase.**

SUN SHADES With their fine, papery petals, Iceland poppies (*Papaver nudicaule*) look fragile, and indeed, they have a short lifespan as cut flowers. However, they make up for this lack of staying power with their gorgeous sunny hues, usually a riotous mixture of yellows, oranges, and reds, often tempered by white. They also have a very graceful form, their hairy stems bending over under the weight of their large blooms. For one arrangement the flowers have been put in a tall, red glass vase; for the other a dark-gray glass vase has been used. However you choose to display them, the result will be cheerful and welcoming—a glimmer of sunshine in any room.

Iceland poppies
require a very
particular and
unusual method
of conditioning if
they're to be used
as cut flowers: the
bottom of the stems
need to be briefly
seared with a flame.

This page **Gerberas are such cheerful flowers to have around the house; their large, open blooms strike a positive note.** Opposite **Using a cocktail of strong colors requires confidence, but the results can be uplifting, especially when the display is set against the neutral backdrop of a white wall.**

BRIGHT SPARKS This display of mid-pink and sunny yellow gerberas (*Gerbera*) couldn't be easier to create. Glass phials, now widely available, can be stuck on a wall where the flowers can be enjoyed at close quarters—by the kitchen sink, as here, or perhaps on a bathroom mirror. Since few stems are used, the flowers can be changed regularly at minimal cost. Poppy anemones (*Anemone coronaria* De Caen Group) or carnations (*Dianthus*) would make good substitutions.

Opposite, more vibrant gerberas, this time arranged in a Fifties steel bowl with a black exterior and red interior. Rather than cutting the stems level with the rim of the bowl, the flowers have been left long and anchored with the use of a pin holder to give the display a more structured look.

RICH PICKINGS If you're unsure how to combine colors
yourself, it's simpler to buy a bunch that does the job for you.
Opposite, these tightly furled ranunculus (*Ranunculus asiaticus*)
in rose and bright pink, orange, red, and yellow show how well
these hot shades work together. The flowers have been cut to
a uniform length and arranged informally in a simple white china
bowl. Chicken wire, shaped into a dome, was placed in the bowl
and secured with tape to create a framework to hold the stems.
With a small bowl, you may need a pin holder or weight in the
bottom to act as ballast so the flowers don't make it top heavy.

Above and above right, a bold arrangement of sunflowers
(*Helianthus annuus*), lotuses (*Nelumbo*), and cordyline leaves
(*Cordyline*) doesn't compromise the masculinity of this
bedroom. Hot pink and deep yellow are a punchy combination
and create a hot spot of color in this subdued interior.

Combining warm
shades produces a
positive and vibrant
effect. However, if
you're wary of
putting this sort of
scheme together
yourself, you can
begin by buying a
readymade bunch
from a florist.
You may then feel
confident enough
to create your
own delicious
floral medley.

SUMMER ON ICE An ice bowl makes a spectacular dinner party arrangement and isn't as hard to make as it looks. Take a plastic or Pyrex bowl and place a smaller one inside it, then tape across the top of both bowls in a crisscross pattern, making sure the rims of the bowls are level. Tuck flowers, leaves, or fruit down the gap between the bowls and carefully fill with water, then freeze. Here, sprigs of rosemary (*Rosmarinus officinalis*) not only look good, but help to anchor smaller items such as the pink and red rose petals (*Rosa*), which might otherwise float to the top. Summer berries—which also look pretty frozen into an ice bowl—have been piled inside for a delicious dessert. Dark pink tulips and glassware match the sumptuous tones of the berries and help to create a table setting guaranteed to make mouths water.

A gorgeous palette of tempting berry shades helps to set the scene for a beautiful summer feast. Ice bowls look impressive, but are simple to make once you've mastered the basic technique.

natural hues

Above **Echeveria** (*Echeveria*) can be bought as potted plants. Here, they've been split into individual rosettes and their roots washed of soil. They've then been placed in small, plain glasses to create an indoor water garden on a low table. When it's time for a change, a home can be found for the plants in the garden.

NATURAL SELECTION Many shrubs need to be pruned after the summer growth period. Instead of consigning the resulting pile of branches to the bonfire, keep the best and put them to stylish use. Opposite and top left, an earthenware vase holds an arrangement of bare branches whose intricate tracery is highlighted by the neutral background. This is the ultimate in low-maintenance floristry: you don't need to add any water to the container, and the result will last all winter.

Above, this collection of pebbles, candles, and plants on a mantelpiece makes a beautiful still life. The smaller vase holds St. John's wort berries (*Hypericum*). Ivy (*Hedera helix*) has been coiled inside the cylindrical vase and pears placed in the bottom.

SPRING STILL LIFE Pussy willow (*Salix caprea*) comes into flower in spring and is a familiar sight in the countryside, although it can also be bought from florists. The stems, covered in trademark furry nodules, are supple enough to be bent and coiled, giving the idea for this sculptural display.

A bunch of long stems, bound at the base with florist's wire and anchored using a pin holder, has been placed in a square aluminum dish. More stems have been coiled into a circle and secured with florist's wire. As an optional extra, a few heads of dyed yellow amaryllis (*Amaryllis*) have been tucked into the display to add a touch of vibrancy. Placed on a low coffee table, the stems have a simplicity reminiscent of oriental flower arrangements.

Right **Fresh dyed flowers, such as these yellow amaryllis, can be bought at some florists. The technique involves submerging cut stems in dye, which is drawn up by the plant to tint the petals. Dyed flowers are often very bright, so they're useful for times when you want to make a bold statement or just have a bit of fun.**

flower care and conditioning

• When you're buying flowers, take the time to make sure that those you're choosing are of good quality, with healthy foliage and strong stems, so they will give you a beautiful display for the maximum amount of time. This is particularly important with very simple arrangements, when the flowers really have to speak for themselves.

• Flowers in bud when bought or gathered from the garden will give the longest display and will also give you the pleasure of watching them come into full bloom. Commercially grown flowers are usually specially treated to prolong their lifespan. Most fresh flowers should last five days or more, and those available in supermarkets are often guaranteed to bloom for a certain number of days.

• If you're buying flowers from a florist, don't be afraid to ask for advice—they ought to be knowledgeable about their stock and happy to help with any questions you may have.

• If you're cutting flowers from your own garden, carry a container of water around with you into which you can immediately plunge the cut stems. This will prevent them from drying out before you get them inside and into their own vase or container.

• Remember that with annual flowers, the more you harvest them, the more blooms they'll produce, so don't be afraid to cut them regularly. You may even want to grow some plants specially for arrangements in the house. If you're an inexperienced gardener, choose packets of seed that state "hardy annual," which means they can be sowed straight into the soil following the instructions on the pack.

• When you get your cut flowers home, take at least ½ inch/2cm off the bottom of the stems with a pair of sharp scissors or shears, cut on an angle to help maximize their absorption of water.

• Before arranging your flowers, give them a good, long drink in deep water to firm up

the stems and help them last longer—they'll absorb half the water they need in the first 24 hours.

• Most purchased bunches of flowers come with a sachet of plant food. It's well worth using and will prolong the life of your flowers. If you're using plants from the garden, florists also suggest adding sugar, lemonade, or aspirin to the water to keep your flowers looking healthy longer.

• If you're using material with woody stems, such as branches of blossom, smash the ends with a hammer or rolling pin to help them to take up water.

• If you're using carnations, cut them just above a leaf nodule.

• Leave daffodils in water overnight to remove excess sap before arranging.

• If you're using Iceland poppies, leave the stems uncut, or if you cut them, singe the ends with a flame. Otherwise, they will exude a milky sap.

• Strip stems of leaves where they'll be below the water line, or they'll become slimy and cloud the water. In any case, it's a good idea to remove some of the leaves so they're not competing with the stems for water.

• Use tepid water in which to arrange your flowers because oxygen travels more readily through warm water, and therefore up the plant's stems, than it does through cold water.

• Some cut flowers, such as gerberas, love-lies-bleeding, and dill, benefit from having their stems plunged into boiling water before being arranged.

• Some flowers, such as violets, are less likely to flag if they are submerged in cool water overnight before being arranged. You can keep them looking fresh by spritzing the arrangement frequently with cold water.

• To maximize the life of your flowers, keep the water crystal clear. This means changing the water regularly—probably every other day—and keeping your containers squeaky clean.

• Some of the longest-lasting flowers are chrysanthemums, carnations, hydrangeas, roses, and calla lilies. Dahlias, sweet peas, and anemones are among those that don't last as well.

• To keep your arrangement looking good, remove dead flower heads and leaves when they appear.

• Think twice about displaying tulips in a mixed arrangement. The acidity in tulips can shorten the life of other blooms.

• If you're arranging scented flowers, they'll release their perfume better in a warm room than a cold one.

• Tropical leaves often have a sticky sap on their surface which you can remove by wiping them or dipping them in water.

• If you're using lilies, remove the stamens to prevent their pollen staining anything.

index

sources

US SOURCES

ABC Carpet and Home
For a store near you, call 561 279 7777
www.abchome.com
Exotic collection of design accessories.

Anthropologie
www.anthropologie.com
Quirky vintage-style vases.

The Conran Shop
407 East 59th Street
New York, NY 10022
212 755 9079
www.conran.com
Cutting-edge designer pieces.

Crate & Barrel
www.crateandbarrel.com
Good-value accessories.

IKEA
www.ikea.com
Home basics at great prices.

LSA International
www.lsa-international.co.uk
Glass and porcelain vases.

Macy's
www.macys.com
A wide selection of vases.

MOMA Design Store
44 West 53rd Street
New York, NY 10022
800 447 6662
www.momastore.org
A selection of accessories by
modern designers.

Pier One Imports
www.pier1.com
Great home accessories.

Pottery Barn
www.potterybarn.com
Good range of decorative accessories.

Restoration Hardware
www.restorationhardware.com
Funky home accessories.

Target Stores
www.target.com
Vases both funky and functional.

UK SOURCES

Alfie's Antiques Market
13–25 Church Street
London NW8 8DT
020 7723 6066
www.alfiesantiques.com
Vintage glassware and ceramics.

Atelier Abigail Ahern
137 Upper Street
London N1 1QP
www.atelierabigailahern.com
Hand-thrown bowls and mouth-blown glass
vases.

Brissi
196 Westbourne Grove
London W11 2RH
020 7727 2159
www.brissi.co.uk
Glass and ceramic vases.

Conran Shop
Michelin House
81 Fulham Road
London SW3 6RD
020 7589 7401
www.conran.co.uk
Cutting-edge designs.

Designers Guild
267 Kings Road
London SW3 5EN
020 7351 5775
www.designersguild.com
Some hand-crafted ceramics.

Dotmaison
www.dotmaison.com
Good for clear glass vases in every shape
and size.

Graham & Green
4 Elgin Crescent
London W11 2HX
020 7243 8908
www.grahamandgreen.co.uk
A variety of different styles.

Habitat
www.habitat.net
Good-value, trend-led vases.

Heal's
www.heals.co.uk
Classic and contemporary styles.

Iittala
126 Regent Street
London W1B 2EB
020 7287 5600
www.iittala.com
Scandinavian classics.

Ikea
www.ikea.com
Cheap and cheerful vases.

John Lewis
www.johnlewis.com
Affordable glass and ceramic vases.

LSA International
Visit www.lsa-international.com for details of
your nearest stockist
Practical and beautiful glassware and
ceramics.

Nicole Farhi Home
17 Clifford Street
London W1X 8BY
020 7494 9051
www.nicolefarhi.com
Subtle, elegant ceramics.

Vessel
114 Kensington Park Road
London W11 2PW
020 7727 8001
www.vesselgallery.com
The very best contemporary glass and
ceramic design.

The White Company
www.thewhitecompany.com
Clear glass vases and elegant ceramics.

Zara Home
www.zarahome.com
Good-value vases and containers.

credits

Picture credits

Photography by Polly Wreford

Key: a=above, b=below, r=right, l=left, c=center

Endpapers Karen Nicol and Peter Clark's home in London; 2 Photographer Michael Paul's house in London; 8 a Photographs by photographer Julia Bostock, Painting by Russian Impressionist, Caelt Gallery; 13 r Clare Nash's home in London; 14 Robert Merrett and Luis Peral's apartment in London; 15 a Francesca Mills' house in London; 16 a Emma Greenhill's London home; 22–23 Francesca Mills' house in London; 24 Photographer Michael Paul's house in London; 26 & 30–39 Jo Plismy, Gong; 42–43 Photographer Michael Paul's house in London; 43 br Karen Nicol and Peter Clark's home in London; 44 Jo Plismy, Gong; 45 Photographer Michael Paul's house in London; 46 Clare Nash's home in London; 47 Robert Merrett and Luis Peral's apartment in London; 50 Painting by Mark Upton; 51–52 l Laurent Bayard's home in London; 53 Francesca Mills' house in London; 54 Emma Greenhill's London home; 57 & 59 Francesca Mills' house in London; 64 l Clare Nash's home in London; 67 inset Emma Greenhill's London home; 68 Photographer Michael Paul's house in London; 71 Francesca Mills' house in London; 72 Karen Nicol and Peter Clark's home in London; 73 l Francesca Mills' house in London; 76 & 77 b Laurent Bayard's home in London; 77 a & 80–81 Photographer Michael Paul's house in London; 82 l Laurent Bayard's home in London; 82–83 Emma Greenhill's London home; 84 Photographer Michael Paul's house in London; 86 Robert Merrett and Luis Peral's apartment in London; 90–91 Emma Greenhill's London home; 92–93 Karen Nicol and Peter Clark's home in London, collage artwork by Peter Clark; 94–95 Laurent Bayard's home in London; 96 Clare Nash's home in London; 97 Photographs by photographer Julia Bostock, painting by Russian Impressionist, Caelt Gallery; 98 inset Emma Greenhill's London home; 99 Robert Merrett and Luis Peral's apartment in London; 100–101 Photographer Michael Paul's house in London; 104 Karen Nicol and Peter Clark's home in London; 106 & 110 Francesca Mills' house in London; 111 Robert Merrett and Luis Peral's apartment in London; 112 Clare Nash's home in London; 113 Laurent Bayard's home in London; 114–115 Photographer Michael Paul's house in London; 117 Grey vases by Heather Dodd; 118 Karen Nicol and Peter Clark's home in London, embroidery by Karen Nicol; 120–121 Photographer Michael Paul's house in London

Business Credits

Laurent Bayard
Interiors
+44 (0)20 7328 2022
Pages 51–52 l, 58 l, 76, 77 b, 82 l, 94–95, 113

Peter Clark
Collage Artwork
+44 (0)20 8979 4593
Pages 43 br, 72, 92–93, 104, 118, Endpapers

Gong
172 Fulham Road
LondonSW10 9PR
020 7370 7176
joplismy@hotmail.com
www.gong.co.uk
Pages 26, 30–39, 44

Emma Greenhill
egreenhill@freenet.co.uk
Pages 16 a, 54, 67 inset, 82–83, 90–91, 98 inset

Robert Merrett
Color and Lifestyle consultant
robert.merrett@macunlimited.net
Pages 14, 47, 86, 99, 111

Clare Nash
House Stylist
+44 (0)20 8742 9991
Pages 13 r, 46, 64 l, 96, 112

Karen Nicol Embroidery
www.karennicol.com
Pages 43 br, 72, 92–93, 104, 118, Endpapers

Michael Paul
Photographer
www.michaelpaulphotography.co.uk
Pages 2, 24, 42–43, 45, 68, 77 a, 80–81, 84, 100–101, 114–115, 120–121

Mark Upton
Paintings
+ 44 (0)7931 391635
Pages 28, 50

acknowledgments

Working on *Easy Flowers* has been a very happy experience for me—
a lovely team to work with and some inspiring locations.
Many thanks to Polly Wreford who was both inspired and exciting to work with; her assistant
Matt Wrixon who was always helpful loading and unloading, and feeding me chocolate.
Many thanks to Antonia Swinson for ensuring all the necessary information appeared in the text.
Thanks to the Ryland Peters & Small team, particularly to Gabriella Le Grazie and Luis Peral for
their creative input, and to Annabel Morgan, Sharon Ashman, and Claire Hector.
Special thanks to Claire Durbridge and all those friends who allowed us to invade their homes:
Laurent Bayard, Alex Durbridge, Emma Greenhill, Mike and Kumeko Paul, and Luis Peral.
To everyone in Covent Garden Market, particularly Brian on Porter's Foliage; Charlie Gardner on
Rymark Flowers; and Ian, David, and Tony on Baker Duguid.

Jane Durbridge